DK 24 HOURS
Coral Reef

LONDON, NEW YORK, MUNICH,
MELBOURNE, and DELHI

Written and edited by Caroline Bingham
Senior designer Cathy Chesson
Art editor Laura Roberts

DTP Designer Almudena Díaz
Picture researcher Sarah Pownell
Production Shivani Pandey
Jacket design Chris Drew
Jacket editor Carrie Love
Jacket copywriter Adam Powley

Publishing manager Susan Leonard
Managing art editor Clare Shedden

Consultant Dr. Frances Dipper
With thanks to Lisa Magloff for
project development

First published in Great Britain in 2005 by
Dorling Kindersley Limited
80 Strand, London WC2R 0RL

A Penguin Company

2 4 6 8 10 9 7 5 3 1

Copyright © 2005 Dorling Kindersley Limited

A CIP catalogue record for this book
is available from the British Library.

ISBN 1-4053-0860-5

Colour reproduction by Colourscan, Singapore
Printed and bound in China by L. Rex
Printing Co. Ltd.

Discover more at
www.dk.com

Welcome to our coral reef

6:00 am Dawn

Introduction   page 4
Dawn   page 6
Plankton   page 8
It's getting busy!   page 10
Clever disguises   page 12

9:00 am Morning

Mid-morning   page 14
Parrotfish   page 16
Midday   page 18
Cleaning station   page 20

It is incredible but true that many of a
reef's creatures follow a pattern of behaviour
over **24 hours** that is similar to the pattern
you follow. They eat, sleep, rest, play, and
build homes and shelters. Come and
discover how they live.

It is a fabulous "rainforest of the sea".

2:00 pm Afternoon

6:00 pm Dusk

10:00 pm Night

Early afternoon	page 22	Dusk	page 30	Night	page 38
Anemonefish	page 24	Coral polyps	page 32	Sharks on patrol	page 40
A peep above	page 26	Night creatures	page 34	Midnight	page 42
Sea slugs	page 28	Night curiosities	page 36	Turtle highway	page 44
				Glossary	page 46

Coral reefs cover less than **one** per cent of Earth's surface, and yet are **home** to more than **15** per cent of all fish species.

In 24 hours Coral Reef, you have the opportunity to follow a day and night in the life of the different creatures that live on a reef. At dawn, 10 am, 2 pm, dusk, and 10 pm, we also return to the same five animals, shown on this page, to see what they are doing.

Green turtle

The green turtle is one of the world's largest sea turtles. Turtles use their front flippers to pull themselves through the water and their back flippers to steer. They cannot breathe underwater, and frequently visit the surface for air.

Titan triggerfish

Our reef is home to the largest of all triggerfish, the titan triggerfish. It can grow to 75 cm (30 in) long. If nesting, this fish can be aggressive towards divers, chasing them out of its territory and giving a nasty bite. Divers are wary of them.

Moray eel

The moray eel is shaped like a snake, but with long fins running the length of its body. It's well over 1 m (3 ft) long. Its day is spent in a small cave in the coral reef, from where it will ambush passing prey if it gets the chance. It can swim free, but usually only does this at night.

Scale As you read 24 hours Coral Reef, look for scale guides. These are based on children who are about 115 cm (3 ft 9 in) tall and provide a guide to the size of some of the creatures you will meet.

Now you see it, now you don't!

8:02 am Coral reefs are full of colour and movement, but things can change in an instant. Look out for time sequences.

Whitetip reef shark

It is easy to identify this shark because it has a white tip on its dorsal fin and on the top tip of its tail. It is also known as the "blunthead". It can grow to be more than 2 m (6.5 ft) in length.

Bubble coral

Bubble coral is a hard, reef-building coral. Such corals need light because they contain tiny plants called algae that make them extra food. This coral's bubbles expand in the day, allowing the algae to get the most light they can.

1 Moray eel **2** Butterflyfish **3** Turtle
4 Soft coral **5** Hard coral

Dawn has broken over the "rainforest of the sea", the coral reef. Morning is a busy time on the reef as the fish wake up and begin their search for breakfast.

The **moray eel** is resting in his hole. He constantly opens and shuts his mouth, sucking fresh water over his gills to breathe.

The **turtle** is tired and hungry. She has had a busy night, laying more than 100 eggs on the beach. She's heading for the reef for breakfast.

The **triggerfish** has just woken up and emerged from his crevice. He is ready to go off hunting for crunchy crabs and sea snails.

The **bubble coral** senses it's morning because of the change in light. It has begun to expand its bubbles, or vesicles.

The **reef shark** has had a successful night's hunting. With a full tummy, she's now ready for a rest. She's a big fish and smaller fish stay clear.

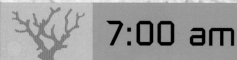
Millions of tiny animals are visible to predators in bright light. During the day, they move down to the darker depths of the sea, because they don't want to be eaten. These are the zooplankton.

Some zooplankton look like miniatures of the adults they will become, like this shrimp larva.

Don't worry! This planktonic lobster larva is magnified 1000s of times.

The bottom of the ladder
Plankton may be small but without them the corals, and other sea life, would not exist. They form the base of the sea's food chain.

"Plankton" comes from a Greek word that means "drifting".

Some plankton have spikes...

Rising to the surface

There are two main types of plankton: phytoplankton and zooplankton. The first are plants. Zooplankton are animals, many of which come up to the sea's surface at night to eat the phytoplankton.

Phytoplankton use sunlight to produce much of the oxygen we breathe.

In close-up

Many plankton are so tiny that they can only be seen properly through a microscope. A drop of sea water may hold 100,000 phytoplankton.

The daytime fish are now very active. They tend to move higher above the coral as the light increases, but are quick to dart back to the safety of holes and crevices in the coral if danger threatens.

There are two main types of corals: hard and soft. **Hard corals** are the reef-building corals and have a protective stony base. Most feed at night. Many **soft corals** feed during the day and sway with the movement of the water. They contribute to the daytime colours of the reef.

A finger-sized squirt can filter a litre (2 pints) of sea water each hour.

Squirt squirt
Sea squirts show little reaction to changes of light. Day and night they suck water in through one tube and squirt it out of another.

Soft corals tend to grow on overhangs and cliffs.

Batfish often swim behind turtles, hoovering up the scraps of food the turtles drop. Black stripes across their eyes help to disguise the vulnerable head: the aim is for the predator to attack the tail, so that the batfish can escape.

There are more than 100 different types of butterflyfish. All have beautiful markings.

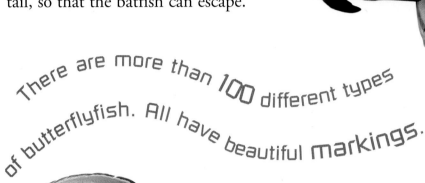

Like many reef fish, **butterflyfish** have flattened bodies, perfect for nipping in between the corals. Butterflyfish indicate the health of a reef. The greater the number and variety, the healthier the reef. Butterflyfish often swim in pairs.

It's difficult to see, but a fierce battle is taking place on the reef. **Corals** are always competing for space and light, as are simple reef animals called **sponges**. It can be a battle to the death when one grows over the other.

Corals are animals. Hard corals settle on the sea floor, and on slopes.

11

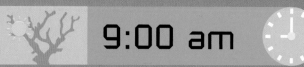
Some fish don't need to hide, even in the bright light of morning. In fact, many fish have odd but effective ways of making sure they don't become a bigger fish's snack. Some have poisonous stings, while others are just so well camouflaged that they are very difficult to spot.

A large lionfish may come out in the daytime.

Lionfish spines contain poison and predators learn to avoid them. A lionfish sting can stop a fish moving or even kill it. It can be dangerous for humans, too.

Who's hiding in a crevice? With its long spines, this **porcupine fish** would make a painful meal. It will begin to hunt at night. If threatened, it can expand into a spiky ball.

The aptly named **boxfish** is an awkward swimmer because it is covered in bony plates that form a tough armour. Not only that, its skin releases a poisonous mucus.

Frogfish are able to change their colour.

This spongy-looking creature is a **frogfish**. It's a hard fish to spot, which makes it a good hunter. It can open its mouth – wide – and suck in a tasty fish in a flash.

An unwary catfish becomes breakfast.

Who's lurking on the bottom? The creepy-looking **crocodile fish** is a clever hunter. It stays dead still. Then, with a snap, a passing fish – or perhaps a crab – is sucked in. It has no warning of its fate.

1 Hard coral **2** Shoaling jacks **3** Turtle

W**ith the** Sun's rays lighting up the sea, the fish know they are easy targets for a tasty snack. So some group together, seeking the protection of huge schools.

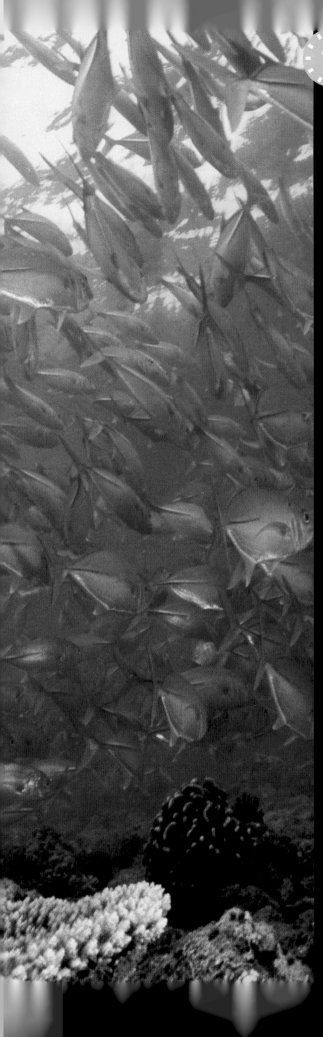

From the safety of his hole, the **moray eel** opens his mouth wide, showing a set of needle-sharp teeth. He can give a nasty bite to an unwary diver.

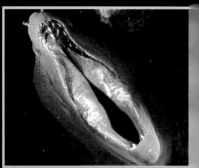

The **turtle** has just popped up to get some air. When awake and moving around, turtles can stay under the water for about 5 minutes.

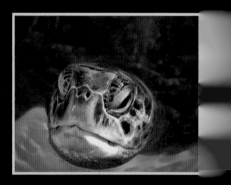

The **triggerfish** has found his breakfast. He is tackling a prickly sea urchin by flipping the urchin over and attacking the underside.

Now fully expanded, it's easy to see how the **bubble coral** gets its name. The delicately-patterned bubbles hide the coral's skeleton.

The **reef shark** is still resting. Unlike many sharks, she does this by staying in one place on the bottom.

Bumphead parrotfish spend their days grazing in groups.

Is coral tasty? Parrotfish think so. Having rested all **night**, they are now hungry and head for the **coral**. The world's largest parrotfish, the bumpheads, use their heads to loosen bits of coral to eat.

There are about 80 different types of parrotfish. All are very colourful. ....

CRUNCH

16

Parrotfish take their name from their bright colours, their flapping fins, and their beaks.

From fish to beach

Parrotfish grind down the rocky coral they eat and pass it out as sand. It's amazing, but true, that in this way just one parrotfish creates many kilograms (pounds) of sand each year – sand that finds its way to tropical beaches.

Parrotfish are grazers, and scrape small plants called algae off corals. Bumpheads eat the coral too.

Bony beak

A parrotfish's beak is made of fused teeth. It is an ideal tool for chiselling away at the reef. Parrotfish are sometimes called the "cows of the sea".

17

Midday and the burning Sun is overhead. The promise of a lazy afternoon washes over the reef. The morning rush is over, and there's plenty of time to look at a few of the giants of the reef: the curiously-shaped sponges, the giant manta ray, and the amazing giant clam.

The **barrel sponge** may look like a plant, but sponges are simple animals. Sponges are covered in tiny holes through which they draw in water, taking out the food and oxygen they need. Barrel sponges can grow to reach a metre (3 ft) in height.

Sponges cannot move, unlike most animals. They feed on tiny particles of food.

Mouth

With a lazy flap of its wing-like fins, a **giant manta** glides slowly by. From wingtip to wingtip, these creatures can be as wide as a small aeroplane.

Manta rays are filter feeders, scooping in plankton-rich sea water. These gentle giants can live for about 20 years.

It's a metre (3 ft) across and very heavy.

Many people see molluscs every day in the form of slugs and snails. The **giant clam** is also a mollusc. By midday, the clam's shell is wide open, exposing its fleshy lips to the sunlight.

19

It's early afternoon and time for a wash and brush-up at the local cleaning station.

A cleaner shrimp's antennae are ideal for probing.

Cleaner wrasse perform a bobbing dance to advertise their services as cleaners.

Cleaning stations do big business on the daytime reef. It's a place where fish and turtles go to get cleaned up.

Table coral provides a good platform for a cleaning station's queue.

Ready for a clean-up

1:10 pm A coral trout is waiting in the queue for the cleaning station. This large predator will not eat the shrimp that cleans it of parasites.

1:15 pm The trout keeps its mouth wide open while it is being cleaned. It stays motionless to let the cleaner know it will not be harmed.

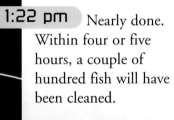

1:22 pm Nearly done. Within four or five hours, a couple of hundred fish will have been cleaned.

Cleaners are fast workers.

I'll do the mouth!

A pair of blue-streak cleaner wrasse are busy cleaning away parasites inside the mouth and gills of a big fish called a sweetlips.

2:00 pm

1 Turtle   **2** Sea fir   **3** Manta ray

By 2 pm the reef is a little quieter. The daytime animals have had their breakfast and lunch, and the night-time animals are still resting. Small fish ignore the passing manta ray, still busy scooping up plankton.

The **moray eel** is taking his turn at the cleaning station. Morays are messy eaters and they need cleaning frequently.

The **turtle** is nibbling sea grass. Adult green turtles spend lots of their time eating sea grass, mangrove roots, and leaves.

The **triggerfish** is tending to his eggs, and is keeping them clean by blowing sand away. He also blows sand to uncover hidden animals.

A close look at the **bubble coral** reveals tiny creatures living amongst the safety of its bubbles – like this little shrimp.

The **reef shark** has found a deep crevice in which to hide. She's still resting – she won't be very active until the Sun goes down.

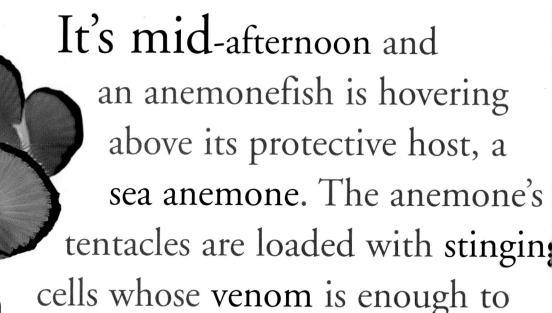

It's mid-afternoon and an anemonefish is hovering above its protective host, a sea anemone. The anemone's tentacles are loaded with stinging cells whose venom is enough to keep most fish away. Not so anemonefish, which have a protective coat of slime.

Anemone-fish

Some sea anemones close up into a tight ball if threatened.

24

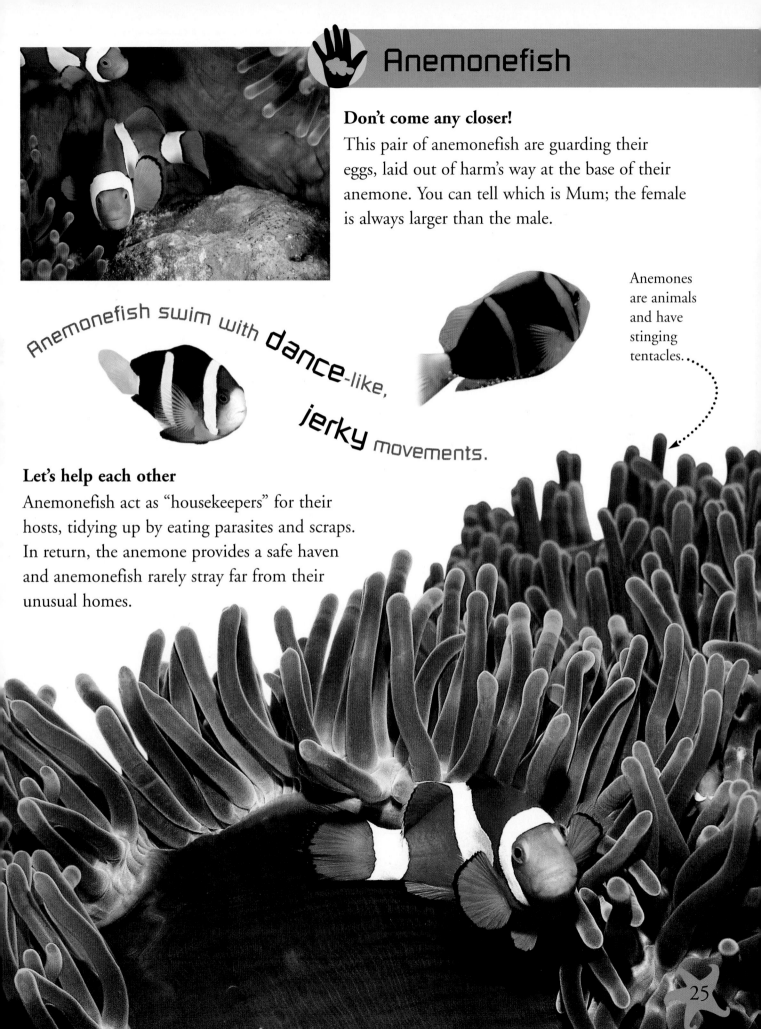

Don't come any closer!

This pair of anemonefish are guarding their eggs, laid out of harm's way at the base of their anemone. You can tell which is Mum; the female is always larger than the male.

Anemones are animals and have stinging tentacles.

Anemonefish swim with dance-like, jerky movements.

Let's help each other

Anemonefish act as "housekeepers" for their hosts, tidying up by eating parasites and scraps. In return, the anemone provides a safe haven and anemonefish rarely stray far from their unusual homes.

Our coral reef, like many other reefs, surrounds a small, low-lying **island**. The island may be tiny, but it is home to a wide **variety** of birds, mammals, and reptiles.

26

A paradise for birds

The island is a good base for birds. Herons and egrets stalk the shores, feeding on fish from the reef. Other birds enjoy the insects and fruits that are found on the island.

Life on the island

Monitor lizards are meat eaters, and will eat almost anything they find. This one is eating a clutch of turtle eggs.

Coconut crabs are big! They are also called robber crabs because they sometimes pinch campers' gear, such as batteries or bottles.

The island's fruit bats love sweet, juicy fruit, but also sip nectar from flowers. They tend to feed at night and sleep in the day.

With their bold feathers, Nicobar pigeons are probably the prettiest pigeons in the world. They feed on insects, seeds, and berries.

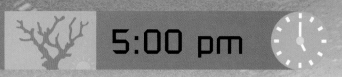
Many sea slugs are smaller than your middle finger.

The Sun is now low in the sky, and a colourful collection of sea slugs are grabbing a late afternoon bite. Unlike their drab, land-based cousins, sea slugs brighten up the reef with a **kaleidoscope** of patterns. Many different varieties can be seen on our reef.

The bright colours shout, **"I'm poisonous. Don't touch!"**

Most slugs feed during the day and rest at night.

Grub's up

Sea slugs are carnivores, meaning that they eat animals not plants. They love to munch on sponges or soft corals, and different types are fussy about which food they will eat.

Sea slugs breathe through external gills.

Sea slugs are solitary animals, but can sometimes be found in small groups.

What's that?

Believe it or not, sea slugs lay eggs! Most lay them in a long, coiled ribbon and the eggs are protected from predators and bacteria by a jelly-like substance that joins the eggs.

 6:00 pm

Dusk is a dangerous time for the coral fish, as their silhouettes are highlighted by the setting Sun. There's a lot of activity, with some fish heading for bed and others just waking up.

1 Lionfish **2** Scuba diver **3** Reef shark
4 Anemone

The **moray eel** has left his hole and is swimming free. He is now hungry, and dusk is a perfect time for him to hunt.

The **turtle** is looking for a place to sleep. She will soon settle down and, when not moving, can stay underwater for a couple of hours.

The **triggerfish** is relaxing and being cleaned near his nest by a cleaner wrasse. But if a diver disturbs him, he will attack.

The **bubble coral** has reacted to the darkening seas and its bubbles are disappearing, to be replaced by tentacles. It is beginning to feed.

The **reef shark** is cruising along the reef edge. She is looking for an easy meal in the end-of-day rush-hour, but she will ignore the diver.

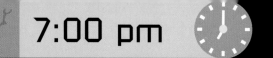

As **night** falls, the hard corals are transformed into a mass of waving tentacles. Coral reefs are made up of millions of tiny animals called polyps. In each coral the polyps, which look like tiny anemones, are joined together.

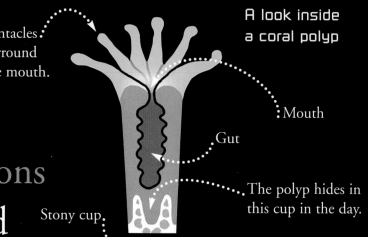

A look inside a coral polyp

Tentacles surround the mouth.

Mouth

Gut

The polyp hides in this cup in the day.

Stony cup

This staghorn coral has extended its tentacles to feed.

This coral is home to a group of brittlestars. Brittlestars are similar to starfish.

Two butterflyfish nestle in a crevice.

Yellow walls

Tubastrea is a coral that thrives in dark, sheltered places on a reef. It fills the reef walls with a wash of yellow at night, when the tentacles extend to catch passing plankton.

It only takes a minute

Before

Each of the hard coral polyps has spent the day in stony cups. The cups help to protect the soft-bodied polyps.

After

After sunset, the polyps extend their tentacles. Blink and you may miss this. They will spend the night feeding.

Each polyp's tentacles are covered in stinging cells.

33

It's well into the night and some of the more
unusual creatures have begun to appear. A cone shell has crawled
out of a coral crevice, while a reef crab picks
about for food. A ghost pipefish drifts silently
past two brightly coloured mandarin fish.

Harlequin ghost pipefish are strange-looking fish covered in tassles. This disguise makes them difficult to spot as they usually hide amongst the frilly arms of featherstars or corals. This pipefish swims with its head down.

They may be beautifully patterned, but **mandarin fish** secrete a disgusting, sticky mucus. A fish that fancies a bite of mandarin for tea won't make the same mistake twice.

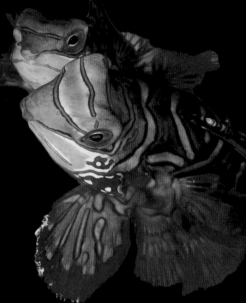

Reef crabs come out to hunt at night, but will scurry to a crevice if threatened. This particular type of reef crab is sometimes known as the "seven-eleven" crab because it has seven large spots and four smaller spots (including its eye spots).

This colourful tube is used to sniff out the cone shell's prey.

There are hundreds of different types of **cone shells** and they are found all over the world. These animals shoot out a "harpoon", or special tooth, from their mouth that injects a powerful poison. This quickly paralyses its victim. They are deadly poisonous to humans – never pick one up.

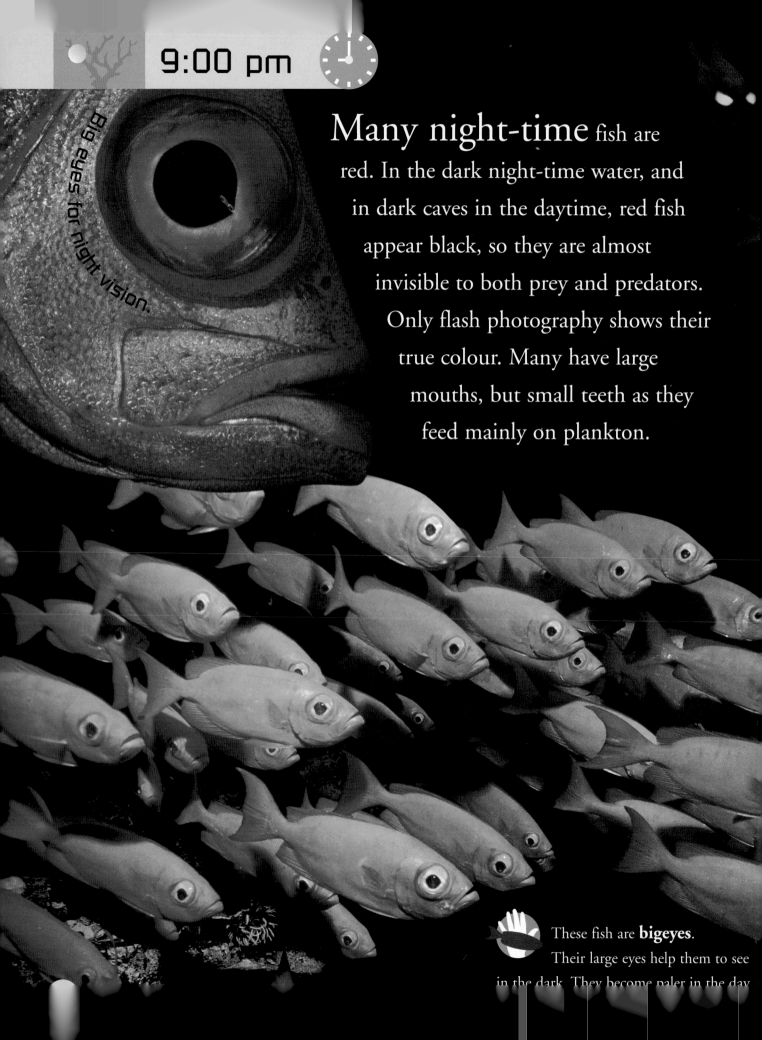

Big eyes for night vision.

Many night-time fish are

red. In the dark night-time water, and in dark caves in the daytime, red fish appear black, so they are almost invisible to both prey and predators. Only flash photography shows their true colour. Many have large mouths, but small teeth as they feed mainly on plankton.

These fish are **bigeyes**. Their large eyes help them to see in the dark. They become paler in the day

The winking lights are used to signal other fish and to confuse predators.

Some fish, such as these **flashlight fish,** can make their own light with the help of bacteria. Flashlight fish live deep down, but rise higher on moonless nights. They can switch off their light by covering it with a skin flap.

Appearance of a Christmas tree

Before This worm has been startled, probably by the photographer, and has withdrawn.

After The worm senses that any danger has gone, and slowly unfolds its pretty tentacles once more.

Christmas tree worms emerge night and day to feed on plankton. They stay in one place for life.

1 Long-spined sea urchin 2 Glassfish
3 Featherstar 4 Double-toothed soldierfish

It is late and the night-time fish have taken over the reef. Tiny glassfish create a flash of shimmering silver, while a small shoal of soldierfish feast on the plankton that have risen higher in the water.

The **moray eel** has seized his chance and ambushed an unwary fish. He will swallow the fish whole, just like a land snake feeds.

The **turtle** has been sleeping on a ledge. She now needs to swim up and take a few gasps of air. Then she will settle down again.

The **triggerfish** is near his crevice. For extra safety he can wedge himself in by locking his "trigger", a strong spine in his dorsal fin.

During the night, the **bubble coral** sometimes withdraws all its tentacles, as well as its bubbles, revealing its hard skeleton.

The **reef shark** has been joined by others. They will swim over the reef during the night, hunting for fish, and will strike with lightning speed.

It is now deep into the night and sharks are swimming back and forth over the reef, hunting for food. One of the strangest-looking sharks of all is the hammerhead.

The largest hammerheads grow to more than 4 m (13 ft) in length.

Why "hammerhead"?
It is thought that the hammerhead's unusual head shape helps this shark sense its prey's position in the water. Sharks do this by picking up small electrical signals that the victim sends out as it moves.

A sea of sharks

Sharks tend to hunt at night in packs and with hammerheads this can be groups of one hundred or more individuals. They look for fish, lobsters, stingrays, and crabs. If one is successful, there might be a feeding frenzy.

The ray must watch out!

Stingrays have venomous spines near the tip of their tail – but this will not stop a hammerhead shark.

Midnight, and many fish and other creatures are fast sleep or resting. This can be a fairly quiet time on the reef, but some night-time fish remain active, still feeding under cover of darkness. Restless predators still prowl around and most small fish stay hidden. Let's take a look around our reef and see what is happening.

Some types of **parrotfish** make a sleeping bag from mucus and spend the night inside. This helps to protect them as it stops predators from picking up their smell.

The **turtle** has to travel to the surface for air every two or three hours, but is otherwise remaining very still. As it sleeps, its eyes will close.

Pinpricks of light occasionally dot the darkened waters. These are because of the tiny, single-celled *Noctiluca*, or **seasparkle**. Under a microscope, *Noctiluca* look like tiny balloons. They sparkle when disturbed.

The big-finned **reef squid** is hunting. This is a well-practised hunter and once it has caught a fish it will chop it up in its strong, beak-like jaws.

The ten tentacles have suckers for grasping prey.

The patchwork-patterned **longnose hawkfish** is a master of disguise. From a distance it can barely be seen against the branching structure of a sea fan.

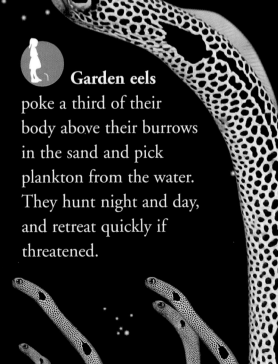

Garden eels poke a third of their body above their burrows in the sand and pick plankton from the water. They hunt night and day, and retreat quickly if threatened.

It's the quiet hours before sunrise, but there's a busy stream of traffic on the reef's island. Hundreds of baby turtles are scrambling towards the sea, having hatched from their eggs. The eggs were laid some 60 days earlier by the turtles' 25-year-old mum.

Sixty days earlier ...

2:00 am The mother turtle had dragged herself up the beach and dug a hole for her eggs. It took her a couple of hours to do this.

4:00 am The mother laid about 100 eggs, then covered them up to protect them.

...break through!

I'll come out now!

A baby turtle uses a special egg tooth to nip its way out of its soft, leathery egg shell. It can then take the babies a couple of days to dig their way out of their sandy nest.

The babies head for the sea as fast as they can.

Artificial light can make some babies head the wrong way. They are under immediate threat from ghost crabs, seabirds, and lizards.

From dawn to dusk

It's a busy time in the morning,

Clock

Butterflyfish

Batfish

Boxfish

Damselfish

Basslets

Crocodile fish

Starfish

Parrotfish

Giant manta

Glossary

Here are the meanings of some of the important words you will come across as you read about coral reefs and the creatures that live there.

ALGAE Simple plants that grow mainly in water.

ANEMONE An animal with a bag-like body and stinging tentacles.

CLEANING STATION A place on a reef that fish visit to be cleaned of parasites.

CORAL Corals are animals made up of tiny individuals called polyps, which all join together. Hard corals have a stony skeleton and they are the ones that form coral reefs.

CREVICE A gap between corals or between rocks.

DAWN The time at the beginning of the day when the Sun rises.

DUSK The time at the end of the day when the Sun sets.

EGG TOOTH A temporary tooth used by baby turtles and other reptiles to break out of their eggs. The tooth drops off soon after the turtle is born.

FEATHERSTAR This is an animal and is related to starfish. It captures plankton with its many arms.

FOOD CHAIN This shows the link between animals through the foods they eat. For example, plankton are eaten by shrimp, and the shrimp are eaten by fish, which are then eaten by larger animals – including human beings.

GILLS The parts of a fish that absorb oxygen from the water and so allow the animal to breathe underwater.

HATCH The moment a baby bird or turtle breaks out of its shell.

PARASITE A creature that lives in or on another organism, the host, causing it harm and sometimes death.

PHYTOPLANKTON Tiny plants that drift in water. They live near the surface, as they use light to make their food.

PLANKTON Plants and animals that drift in water. Most can only be seen with a microscope.

quiet in the middle of the day, and busy again at dusk.

Bigeye fish

Reef squid

Cleaner wrasse

Green turtle

Cleaner shrimp

Sea slug

Garden eels

Reef crab

Ghost pipefish

Cone shell

POISON If a poison is eaten it will cause illness or death.

POLYP A simple animal with a mouth that is surrounded by stinging tentacles.

PREDATOR An animal that hunts another.

SEA FIR This branching animal looks like a plant. It is related to anemones and corals.

TENTACLE A long arm used by some animals to catch their food. Anemones and corals have many stinging tentacles.

VENOM This is a poison that is injected when a victim is stung.

ZOOPLANKTON Tiny animals that drift in water. Some can move up or down in the water.

Picture credits

The publisher would like to thank the following for their kind permission to reproduce their photographs:
(Key: a-above; c-centre; b-below; l-left; r-right; t-top)
Alamy Images: Fabrice Bettex 4c, 7cr, 39cr; James D Watt/Stephen Frink Collection 40-41; S.C. Bisserot/Worldwide Picture Library 27crb. **Ardea.com:** Valerie Taylor 39tr. **Jon Bondy:** 15crb, 31crb, 39crb. **Corbis:** 24cla, 25b; Amos Nachoum 37br; Bob Abraham 3tl, 23tl; Brandon D. Cole 23crb; Darrell Gulin 26cl; Douglas P. Wilson/Frank Lane Picture Agency 43tl; Jeffrey L. Rotman 7crb, 43bl; Kevin Schafer 45tl; Lawson Wood 17tl, 28-29cb, 29br, 33tr, 38bl, 42; Martin Harvey 27br; Robert Yin 10tl, 10c; Stephen Frink 2tl, 4bl, 5bl, 6bl, 7br, 24bl, 40b; Stuart Westmorland 24cr, 25car; Tom Brakefield 15cra. **Dr Frances Dipper:** 37clb, 37bl. **FLPA - images of nature:** Chris Newbert/Minden Pictures 12cra, 13cl; Norbert Wu/Minden Pictures 3tr, 26-27, 38cal, 39bl, 42tr, 43tr; Shin Yoshino/Minden Pictures 27cl. **Getty Images:** David Hall 41tr; Gary Bell 41br. **Image Quest Marine:** 2003 James D. Watt 23br; Roger Steene 15cr, 31cr; Scott Tuason 15br. **N.H.P.A.:** B. Jones & M. Shimlock 26bl. **National Geographic Image Collection:** David Doubilet 37t. **Nature Picture Library Ltd:** Georgette Douwma 43br. **Oceanwide Images:** Gary Bell 1, 2tl, 2b, 3b, 4-5c, 5cra, 6tl, 6-7, 10-11, 10l, 18-19b, 18-19t, 19tl, 19br, 21tl, 21tr, 21cla, 21cl, 30bl, 30cbl. **OSF/photolibrary.com:** 31tr; Dave Fleetham 34br, 35cl; Tobias Bernhard 15tr. **Science Photo Library:** Alexis Rosenfeld 44clb, 44bl; Georgette Douwma 23cr, 27cra; Matthew Oldfield, Scubazoo 3tr, 38tl, 38-39. **Sue Scott:** 11b, 32br, 33cl, 33clb, 33br. **Scubazoo.com:** Jason Isley 2tl, 3tc, 5cb, 7tl, 13br, 31cra, 31cl, 31br, 34, 39br. **Seapics.com:** David B. Fleetham 7cra, 12, 25tl; Doug Perrine 2tr, 3tl, 11tr, 14tl, 14-15, 16tl, 16-17, 17r, 20-21c, 20b, 21b, 22tl, 22-23, 23cra, 25cl, 27tr, 32bl, 39cra, 44tl, 44-45; Franco Banfi 20tr; Gary Bell 9b; James D. Watt 12bl, 13tl, 35cra; Mark Strickland 34bl, 35br; Peter Parks/iq-3d 8tr, 8bl, 9c; Randy Morse 8-9t; Reinhard Dirscherl 4tc, 16r, 18tr, 36tl, 36b, 48b; Shedd Aquar/Ceisel 37cr. **Sub Aqua Images/Fredy J. Brauchli:** 7tr, 12cla, 12br, 13tr, 13clb, 23tr, 28tl, 28-29b. **Treasure Images:** Eric Madeja 34cla, 35tl. **www.uwphoto.no:** Nils Aukan 16bl, 18bl. **www.wildasia.net:** Terence Lim 2tl, 6crb, 11cl, 29tr, 29cl, 33ca. **Norbert Wu:** 3tc, 30tr, 30-31, 42b.
All other images © Dorling Kindersley
www.dkimages.com

Index

Algae 17

Anemone 22-23

Anemonefish 22-23

Batfish 11

Beaches 17

Bigeyes 36

Boxfish 13

Brittlestars 32

Bubble coral 5, 7, 15, 23, 31, 39

Butterflyfish 11, 33

Christmas tree worm 37

Cleaner shrimp 20

Cleaner wrasse 20, 21

Cleaning station 20-21, 23

Cone shell 34, 35

Coral 10-11, 17, 32, 33

Coral trout 20

Crabs
Coconut 27
Reef 34, 35

Crocodile fish 13

Dawn 6-7

Dusk 30-31

Eggs 23, 25, 27, 29, 44-45

Flashlight fish 37

Frogfish 13

Fruit bat 27

Garden eel 43

Giant clam 19

Giant manta 19

Gills 7, 29

Green turtle 4, 7, 15, 23, 31, 39, 42, 44-45

Hammerhead shark 40-41

Harlequin ghost pipefish 34, 35

Hawkfish 43

Lionfish 13, 30

Mandarin fish 34, 35

Midday 18-19

Monitor lizard 27

Moray eel 4, 7, 15, 23, 31, 39

Mucus 13, 35

Nicobar pigeon 27

Night creatures 34-41

Noctiluca 43

Parasite 21, 25

Parrotfish 16-17, 43

Phytoplankton 9

Plankton 8-9, 33, 37, 38

Polyps 32-33

Porcupine fish 13

Sea slug 28-29

Sea squirt 10

Spines 13

Sponge 18

Squid 43

Stingray 41

Teeth 15, 17

Tentacles 24, 25, 32, 33

Titan triggerfish 4, 7, 15, 23, 31, 39

Whitetip reef shark 4, 7, 15, 23, 31, 39

Zooplankton 8, 9